NOTE TO PARENTS

This well known fairytale has been specially written and
adapted for 'first readers', that is, for children who are just
beginning to read by themselves. However, if your child is
not yet able to read, then why not read this story aloud to him
or her, pointing to the words and talking about the pictures?
There is a word list at the back of the book which identifies
some of the difficult words and explains their meaning
in the context of the story.

Cinderella

retold by Clare Humphreys
illustrated by Gill Guile

Copyright © 1990 by World International Publishing Limited.
All rights reserved.
Published in Great Britain by World International Publishing Limited,
An Egmont Company, Egmont House,
P.O. Box 111, Great Ducie Street,
Manchester M60 3BL.

Printed in DDR.
ISBN 0 7235 4472 7

A CIP catalogue record for this book is available from the British Library.

Cinderella lived in the kitchen.
She had two cruel stepsisters.
They made her do all the work.

One day a special messenger came.
He brought an invitation.
It was for the prince's ball.

Cinderella was sad.
Her stepsisters were very cruel.
"You can't go!" they said.
"You must help us get ready."

Cinderella was left alone.
She sat down by the hearth.
A tear trickled down her cheek.

Suddenly, her fairy godmother appeared.
"You shall go to the ball, Cinderella," she said.

She waved her magic wand.
In a flash, Cinderella's rags had gone.
She had on a lovely ball-gown.

The fairy godmother smiled.
She waved her wand again.
Flash! There was a coach!
And eight grey horses.

"You must be home by midnight,"
said the fairy godmother.
Cinderella set off to the ball.

Cinderella arrived at the palace.
Nobody knew who she was.

She danced with the prince all night.
Cinderella was so happy.
But she forgot all about the time.

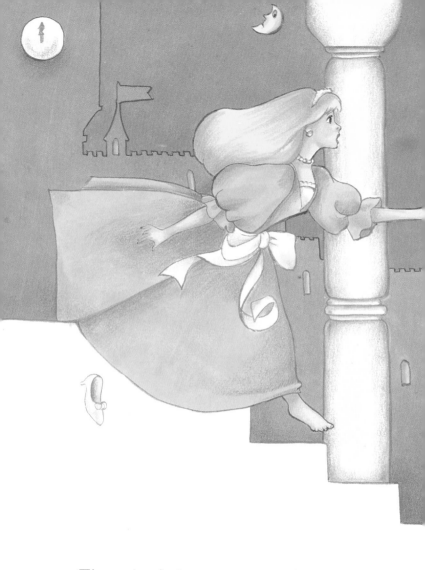

The clock began to strike twelve.
Cinderella ran out of the palace.
One of her slippers fell off.

Cinderella ran all the way home.
She was dressed in rags again.
She was very upset.

The prince found the glass slipper.
He was very happy.
The girl the slipper fitted
would be his true love.

All the ladies of the court
tried the slipper on.
It did not fit any of them.

The prince sent his messengers out.
They had to find the girl whose
foot fitted the slipper.

The ugly sisters heard a fanfare.
They ran out to the messengers.
They wanted to try the slipper on.

The slipper did not fit them.
Cinderella ran forward.
"Please let me try," she said.

The ugly sisters shouted at her.
"Get back to the kitchen," they said.
But one of the messengers gave the
slipper to Cinderella.

The slipper was a perfect fit!
Cinderella smiled.
She felt in her apron pocket.
There was the other slipper.

The ugly sisters could not believe it.
They grabbed Cinderella's foot.
They tried to pull the slipper off.

The messenger told them to stop.
He called the other messenger.
"Go and get the prince," he said.

The prince rode up.
He recognized Cinderella at once.
He leapt down from his horse.

The prince knelt down.
"Please marry me, Cinderella," he said.
The stepsisters wept with anger.

Cinderella went to live in the palace.
She married the prince.
They had a big wedding party.
Even the ugly sisters were invited.

New words

Did you see lots of new words in the story? Here is a list of some hard words from the story, and what they mean.

ball
a very big party with lots of dancing

fanfare
the messenger blew on a trumpet

hearth
the stone floor in front of the fire

invitation
the card asking people to go to the ball

ladies of the court
the ladies who lived at the palace

messenger
the man who gave out the invitations